Amazing Inventions
Inventing Airplanes

by Allan Morey

FOCUS READERS
BEACON

www.focusreaders.com

Focus Readers is distributed by North Star Editions:
sales@northstareditions.com | 888-417-0195

Produced for Focus Readers by Red Line Editorial.

Photographs ©: Shutterstock Images, cover, 1, 4, 6, 10, 13, 14, 17, 19, 20, 23, 25, 26–27, 29; iStockphoto, 8

Library of Congress Cataloging-in-Publication Data
Names: Morey, Allan, author.
Title: Inventing airplanes / by Allan Morey.
Description: Lake Elmo, MN : Focus Readers, [2022] | Series: Amazing inventions | Includes index. | Audience: Grades 2-3
Identifiers: LCCN 2021041742 (print) | LCCN 2021041743 (ebook) | ISBN 9781637390436 (hardcover) | ISBN 9781637390979 (paperback) | ISBN 9781637391518 (ebook) | ISBN 9781637392027 (pdf)
Subjects: LCSH: Airplanes--Juvenile literature. | Aeronautics--History--Juvenile literature. | Aeronautics and civilization--Juvenile literature.
Classification: LCC TL547 .M6723 2022 (print) | LCC TL547 (ebook) | DDC 629.133/34--dc23
LC record available at https://lccn.loc.gov/2021041742
LC ebook record available at https://lccn.loc.gov/2021041743

Printed in the United States of America
Mankato, MN
012022

About the Author

Allan Morey grew up on a farm in central Wisconsin. Some of his first stories were about the animals that lived on the farm. Allan now lives in Minnesota with his wife, dogs, and cats.

Table of Contents

Chapter 1

To the Rescue

Smoke rises into the sky. The forest is burning. But an airplane is on the way to help. The pilot pushes the plane's **control wheel** forward. This tilts the plane's nose. It flies down toward a small lake.

 Some firefighting airplanes dump water on fires. Others drop chemicals.

5

 In 2021, planes could take off and land at more than 41,700 airports around the world.

The plane skims across the lake's surface. Inside the plane, a tank fills with water. Then the pilot pulls back on the control wheel. The plane flies up into the air.

The pilot steers the plane toward the fire. She flies above the flames. Then she releases the water. It puts the fire out.

Fighting fires is just one way people use airplanes. Planes also carry people and **cargo**.

Did You Know?

In the United States, nearly three million people travel by airplane every day.

Chapter 2

History of Airplanes

Humans first took to the air in the 1780s. That is when hot-air balloons were invented. The balloons needed wind to move. They were also hard to steer.

In the 1800s, some people used hot-air balloons to travel.

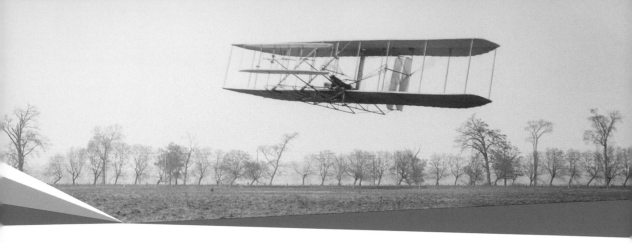

▶ **Early airplane flights by Orville and Wilbur Wright lasted just a few seconds.**

People wanted a more controlled way to fly.

Orville and Wilbur Wright found a solution. The brothers built the world's first airplane. It took flight in 1903. Their plane had two sets of wings. It was made of wood and cloth. It got power from a **propeller** and an engine. This engine burned gasoline as fuel.

Other inventors improved airplane designs. By the 1920s, people began using metal to make airplanes. Some of these planes had just one set of wings. The new designs made the airplanes sturdier.

Did You Know?

Early airplanes had open **cockpits**. Wind and weather hit pilots as they flew.

As a result, the planes could fly higher, faster, and farther. People also worked to improve controls.

In the 1940s, planes began using jet engines. These powerful engines shot out streams of hot gas. They allowed planes to travel faster and farther than ever before.

Did You Know?

Militaries first used airplanes during World War I (1914–1918). Pilots had midair battles called dogfights.

 Two pilots often work together to fly a plane. The cockpit where they sit has computer screens.

By the 1980s, most planes used computers to help pilots fly and steer. In fact, many modern airplanes have autopilot. This system controls the plane's speed, altitude, and direction.

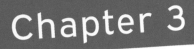

Chapter 3

How Airplanes Work

Airplanes get power from their engines. But the shape of a plane's wings is what helps it fly above the ground. The wings are curved on the top and flat on the bottom.

Some airplanes have a jet engine under each wing.

This shape causes air to move faster over the tops of the wings. This fast air has low **pressure**. Air under the wings moves slower. It has high pressure. This pressure difference creates a force called lift. This force pushes up on the wings and lifts the plane into the air.

Did You Know?

Gliders are aircraft without engines. They depend on lift from their long wings to fly.

 When parts on the wings lift up, more air pushes back against the plane. This slows the plane down.

Pilots use **flaps** on the wings to help control airplanes. Raising and lowering the flaps changes the airflow along the wings. This changes how the plane flies. Flaps can help move the plane up and down. They also help slow the plane as it lands.

Other parts of the wings can move, too. These parts help the plane tilt and turn.

A plane's tail helps keep the plane flying straight through the air. The tail also has moving parts that help pilots steer. The rudder helps control the plane's side-to-side

Did You Know?

Radar is a system that sends out radio waves. When the waves bounce off an airplane, the radar can show the plane's location in the air.

Airplane Parts

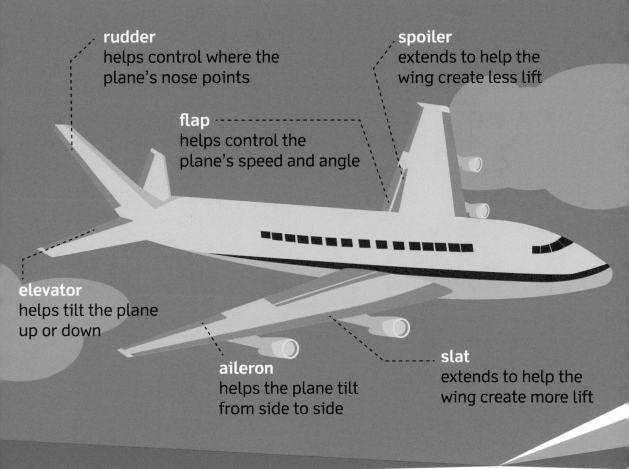

rudder
helps control where the plane's nose points

spoiler
extends to help the wing create less lift

flap
helps control the plane's speed and angle

elevator
helps tilt the plane up or down

aileron
helps the plane tilt from side to side

slat
extends to help the wing create more lift

movement. Elevators control pitch. They tilt the plane's nose up or down.

Chapter 4

Changing Travel

Airplanes changed the way people travel. Long trips by car or train could take days. On a plane, the same trips took hours. It became much easier for people to travel for work or vacation.

 Airplanes make it easier for people to travel long distances.

At first, few people flew. Flying was very expensive, and airplanes were not big enough to carry many passengers. Some of the first commercial airlines were founded in the 1920s. By the 1960s, millions of people were traveling on large jet planes.

Did You Know?

The first airplanes held just the pilot. Modern jets often carry hundreds of passengers.

 Cargo planes have huge spaces inside that can hold many items.

In addition to carrying passengers, airplanes deliver mail and move cargo. Planes can fly quickly across oceans. And they can hold large amounts of cargo.

As a result, sending items around the world is faster and easier than it used to be.

Airplanes also help people do work in places other vehicles can't reach. Some planes help with search and rescue missions. They find people who are lost or hurt. And they quickly bring help.

Other airplanes help scientists do research. Some planes help people study Earth's air and weather. The planes take pictures or collect

> **Some airplanes have floats that let them land on water.**

information. Some planes help people observe wildlife. These planes fly to hard-to-reach places where animals live. People can see the animals from above.

Improving Efficiency

Airplanes create carbon dioxide (CO_2) when they burn fuel. This gas goes into the **atmosphere.** Planes release other gases, too. Together, these gases are a leading cause of **climate change**. So, scientists are looking for ways to help. Some are designing electric airplanes. These planes produce fewer harmful gases. But they aren't as powerful as jet planes. They can't carry as many passengers or as much cargo. Scientists are also working to make jet engines more **efficient**. Using less fuel means they won't produce as much CO_2.

Water vapor from planes can make climate change worse.

FOCUS ON
Inventing Airplanes

Write your answers on a separate piece of paper.

1. Write a sentence describing one way that airplanes have changed people's lives.

2. Would you want to fly in a small airplane made from wood and cloth? Why or why not?

3. Which part of the airplane creates lift?
    A. the wings
    B. the engine
    C. the tail

4. What would happen if an airplane's rudder stopped working?
    A. The pilot would have a hard time steering the airplane.
    B. The airplane would run out of fuel.
    C. The pilot would not be able to control how fast the airplane flew.

5. What does **research** mean in this book?

*Other airplanes help scientists do **research**. Some planes help people study Earth's air and weather.*

    A. learning more about a certain topic
    B. forgetting lots of information
    C. making many loud sounds

6. What does **observe** mean in this book?

*Some planes help people **observe** wildlife. These planes fly to hard-to-reach places where animals live.*

    A. to read a book about something
    B. to go look at something
    C. to stay as far away from something
        as possible

Answer key on page 32.

Glossary

atmosphere
The layers of air that surround Earth.

cargo
Items carried by a vehicle from one place to another.

climate change
A human-caused global crisis involving long-term changes in Earth's temperature and weather patterns.

cockpits
The parts of airplanes where pilots sit.

control wheel
A device in the cockpit that a pilot uses to steer an airplane.

efficient
Able to do a job without using much energy.

flaps
Long, thin metal panels on the backs of airplane wings that can move up and down.

pressure
The amount of force pushing against an object.

propeller
A vertical set of spinning blades that provide thrust, which moves a vehicle forward.

To Learn More

BOOKS

Amstutz, Lisa J. *Airplanes*. Lake Elmo, MN: Focus Readers, 2018.

Bethea, Nikole Brooks. *The First Flight*. Minneapolis: Jump!, 2019.

Oachs, Emily Rose. *The Airplane*. Minneapolis: Bellwether Media, 2019.

NOTE TO EDUCATORS

Visit **www.focusreaders.com** to find lesson plans, activities, links, and other resources related to this title.

Index

Answer Key: 1. Answers will vary; **2.** Answers will vary; **3.** A; **4.** A; **5.** A; **6.** B